GW00993696

DUTY FIRST
Developing Practice with Children and Families Duty Teams

Eva Learner and Gwen Rosen

National Institute for Social Work
on behalf of
Social Care Institute for Excellence

Duty First: Developing Practice with Children and Families Duty Teams

Published 2002
by the National Institute for Social Work
5 Tavistock Place, London WC1H 9SN
www.nisw.org.uk
info@nisw.org.uk
on behalf of the Social Care Institute for Excellence
1st Floor, Goldings House, 2 Hays Lane, London SE1 2HB
www.scie.org.uk
info@scie.org.uk

ISBN 1 899942 44 0

Cover designed by Pat Kahn

Printed by Meridian Print Centre Ltd, Derby

Contents

PREFACE

It is an honour to be asked to write the preface to a book which publishes the conclusions of some of the last of NISW's consultancy work and the first book to be published in the name of the Social Care Institute for Excellence. It is a worthy inheritance, and passes on a tradition of sound advice based fundamentally in the concerns of users and practitioners.

The duty service is the first port of call for families in distress. In many councils the duty team has changed its name to that of referral and assessment team, which accurately describes the work carried out. Whatever the name, all councils need to make sure that their duty systems or referral and assessment systems are working as efficiently and effectively as possible.

This book contains the findings and recommendations of two development consultants who have worked with duty teams to review and improve their standards of practice. Their work has been part of the National Institute for Social Work's practice development programme. Both authors have been working as practice developers in the UK for a number of years and this book synthesises their expertise about how to make the duty service for children and families as safe as possible. Duty social work remains a rather neglected and under-evaluated area of social work practice but its importance is without question.

The findings described in this book have been based largely on local councils where the duty service has been assessed as needing improvement and development. However, the approach and methods advocated are of use to any worker or manager wanting to improve standards of practice in their referral and assessment systems. It will prove helpful to all those who want to improve access for people who need the help of social services.

Denise Platt CBE
Chief Inspector of the Social Services Inspectorate
February 2002

PART ONE: IDENTIFICATION

Section 1: How to use this booklet and who it is for

"Change your opinions, keep to your principles: change your leaves, keep intact your roots."

Victor Hugo (1802-1885)

This booklet has been written to help social work staff who have a responsibility for the duty service in children and families work in a local authority. It will be of interest to those who provide the service on a day-to-day basis; to managers, practitioners and duty team staff who wish to assess, review and develop the duty service; and to social service departments in general who may want to review the service. In addition, service users may find the booklet of interest in respect of the expectations of the service.

The term used in this booklet will be 'duty' team, as being representative of the first-line intake team. The title of duty team is increasingly being referred to as the 'referral and assessment team' in keeping with their function.

Intake social work processed by duty teams has always been important. These teams are the doorway to the service and are responsible for all new referrals, as well as emergency work which must be attended to immediately. With the recent emergence of the Assessment Framework scheme, itself based on practice research findings, the importance of speedy, effective and efficient responses on the intake work at the front-line has been further confirmed. There has been very little published in the way of research and literature for duty work; hence the notion of a booklet offering guidance.

The findings and recommendations of this booklet are based on work undertaken over the past two years, mainly with teams located in disadvantaged areas in central London, but also with teams in outer London and other parts of England and Wales. The writers have worked mostly to support and develop teams overwhelmed with complex problems. In some places children referred for help have been endangered because of the team's inability to respond with an appropriate service. In many places managers and their teams have been able to enhance their services with reorganisation of systems. Other places have had a history of attempts at change with only partial success. A lack of systems, major shortages of staff, and disruption due to long-term sick leave can create difficulties. Some teams have been affected and weakened by departmental restructuring. For certain staff it had been difficult to identify a new mode of working because of the comfort of old habits. Indeed, when work feels so difficult and overwhelming, there is often comfort in chaos. Some of the teams worked with had been assessed by outside organisations such as the Social Services Inspectorate (SSI) and comment had been made with regard to some aspects of their standards of service provision.

Managers tend to be very responsible and very hardworking but often do not have the time or space to think about a positive approach and prepare themselves and the team for reconstruction towards safety and efficiency. This booklet should help both managers and their teams think about and plan improvements in service.

The booklet is set out in sections which are intended to take the reader through the process of reviewing and developing a duty system. Any section can be used on its own but it is suggested that all sections are read by at least one team member in duty and preferably by all staff. Whether the review of duty is to improve current acceptable practice or the more exacting task of changing a poorly-functioning team into one which is fit for the purpose, this booklet will be of interest to you.

This booklet can be used as a guide for all duty staff or as a trigger and aid to the regular review and monitoring of duty, which may be carried out by staff other than those directly involved in the day-to-day delivery of the duty, referral and assessment, or intake service.

Section 2: What is duty work and why is it important?

"Nothing is so exhausting as indecision and nothing so futile."
Bertrand Russell (1872-1970)

Every part of a children and families division in a local authority is integral and vital to the delivery of an appropriate and efficient service. The divisions these days are made up of several special teams that provide a range of social work services to suit particular problems. They are known by various titles like the children in need teams, child protection teams, adoption and fostering teams, children with disability teams, and leaving care or 16-plus teams.

Duty is the first port of call, the front door, or the gateway for both service users and referring organisations. It processes the wide range of referred problems and ultimately determines which particular service team will be appropriate, if indeed a further longer-term service is required. It is important to recognise that the duty team is essentially a team undertaking short-term work with service users.

Access to services has been one of the aims of the Children Act 1989 and local authorities have a duty to advertise services available to the community. This is the general task of departments but duty teams need to consider improving ways of communicating their business to family as well as community based agencies. The latter have intrinsic responsibilities to work together with duty teams. "Families who were seeking help from social services for the first time found it hard to find out which office to go to...there was little available publicity about family support services" (Aldgate and Statham, 2001).

The duty service provides a first assessment of the problem referred and thus, as stated above, identifies the nature of the appropriate service response to the specific needs of the child/family referred. The problem may be resolved immediately within the duty team with various solutions. For example, straightforward information and advice (a social security or housing enquiry, or a child care matter); or a very brief discussion with a social worker can settle a matter of concern (for instance, regarding a difficulty with a child at school, or behaviour problem); or indeed a more intense but brief crisis intervention can settle quite major trouble (for example, with difficult adolescents). Not enough attention is paid to the possibility that parents themselves, if given the opportunity to discuss the options, will resolve the problem themselves within the family – the best solution of all.

Where there are more complex and longer-term problems the child and family may be referred to one of the teams mentioned earlier which undertake longer-term work. At present the Assessment Framework has set standards of assessment which are undertaken at various points in the early referral process in duty. The first point of contact requires the collection of initial information which will then inform a decision as to the nature of the problem and next stage of assessment if it requires a social work service. This will be the Initial Assessment process, which is undertaken in a few days. If the problem appears to reflect the possibility of a child protection matter, the assessment becomes a child protection investigation. This will take the form of a Section 47 investigation (Children Act 1989). Generally these early assessments are undertaken in the duty team.

Hence the duty team sets a standard of service and an expectation; above all it must provide a safety net for children. It is vital that a duty service is as good as it can be. Recent reviews of local authority services by the SSI continue to identify the work in the duty team as a part of the service that in a few cases may be underperforming, and on rare occasions may even be dangerous. A random sample of five Joint Inspections of London local authorities (not the local authorities worked in by the two writers of this booklet) contains the following descriptions of the duty service:

- "Response times vary. Despite some improvement, the child care duty system is still under pressure. There were plans to invest more resources in this."

- "Areas for development: review filtering service between reception and duty teams – achieving more consistency between duty intake and long-term work."

- "High chronic sickness absence levels, slow recruitment, high turnover of manager in the past two years and lack of back-up have all contributed to depressing duty team morale, sometimes leaving administrative staff to cope with no social workers in the mornings."

- "There are persistent differences in the patterns of response between the west and east of the borough. This applies particularly to child protection referrals where there is no policy on risk that is agreed between all relevant agencies."

Thoburn, Wilding and Watson (2000) write "...from what we were told by parents, such contacts (in the first contact with duty staff), helpful or unhelpful, were on occasions seen to have an impact on subsequent attitudes towards contact with social workers."

It is unusual to find the following:

- "Reception and duty arrangements based on experienced and well-trained staff."

Keeping duty practice standards high is important. It is where staff have to make complex and difficult decisions. These may often provide the basis for further and sometimes long-term work with a child and the family. Decisions have to be made with speed but with wisdom and they may have a significant impact on a person's future life. Duty is also an area of social work practice where social workers are in daily contact with a wide variety of family life problems for resolution and help. It is therefore important that the staff who work in duty are prepared, supported and sustained in this demanding area of practice.

Perceptions of the duty service

A number of workers in duty reported feelings of being somewhat marginalised within their organisations. They considered that duty work is sometimes viewed as a second class service, with the real work of the social services department taking place in other long-term social work teams. Duty is sometimes perceived as the 'fill in' or the 'patch up' until service users can be allocated to other teams. In some local authorities, the 'duty' team is now called 'referral and assessment' in order to identify it as the beginning of the social work intervention process rather than a temporary or holding operation. Whatever description is used, it remains a complex and sometimes risky social work service, albeit exceedingly important. The constant demands, the level of stress and the need for rapid response, can work against effective thinking and planning about appropriate social work interventions unless there is a consciously-planned approach.

Targets and outcomes in duty are different from those of the longer-term teams. In the latter, work can be discussed over a longer period, service plans considered and the timescales for work are often months and years rather than the days and weeks of the duty service.

Recent developments – the skills mix

Some local authorities have recently begun to increase the use of non-social work trained staff in the duty team. These workers are most frequently used in the intake or first contact procedure in the duty team. They are less likely to undertake the social work assessment. However, if not seen in context, the employment of these workers could be undermining to qualified social work staff in the team. Sometimes it may be thought that senior management believe that 'anyone' can be used in this work. Although it is every bit as difficult and complex as other social work specialties, we observed that duty teams are, as stated above, not always able to recruit a sufficient number of experienced social workers.

A national problem

The increase in use of non-social work qualified staff is being forced on employers because of the national shortage of qualified social workers. However, the model is interesting and is being tried in several authorities at present. Experienced administrative staff are being used to take the first referral calls on the telephone and/or at the reception desk. In some places there is a mix of these staff along with social work staff; the latter being given referrals which may be immediately recognised to be more complex.

They will on occasion complete the Initial Referral form (not to be confused with the Initial Assessment). At this stage all the basic information is gathered, as well as preliminary checks to see whether the child is already known to the department.

Other staff with degrees in human sciences like sociology, anthropology and psychology are being used in duty teams in the intake or first contact role, as well as family support officers, or social work assistants. Staff with tertiary qualifications in the human sciences, after in-service training, are sometimes used in the duty team to undertake Initial Assessments. Almost always these staff members are given special training in communication skills, awareness of children in need matters and issues of child protection and significant harm. Much of their work is centred on the giving of general advice and information, so topics like welfare rights, housing and immigration are very much a matter of interest to them. They may also be involved in the Assessment Framework training. They are usually very closely supported and monitored. It should be remembered that for many years, unqualified social work staff have been used as family support workers and welfare assistants attached to teams, undertaking long-term work with children and families.

This pattern of a skill mix in duty is also being forced on employers by the decisions of experienced social workers to move from duty into longer-term work such as children in need, or looked after children. These latter teams also sometimes use family support workers or aides. As noted above, some duty teams are making good use of the skills mix, and this is still being tried and tested. It is likely that the use of a mix of qualified social work and unqualified personnel in most local authorities will continue and increase, certainly in the short to medium term. Rather than seeing skill mix as marginalising or second class, it should be viewed as an area of social work practice which is leading the way. If staff are properly inducted, trained and deployed, this could be a more effective and efficient way of delivering the duty service. However, this needs further evaluation and development. An interesting development in some places is the use in the duty teams of specialist workers, expert in information and advice, and covering matters like housing, welfare benefits or asylum seekers. They may not have social work qualifications but can prove a huge asset in appropriate gatekeeping and assessment. They provide speedy and effective resolutions to sometimes very time-consuming non-social work problems. Social services in all big cities (and many smaller towns) are beset with housing or social security problems which do not need a qualified social worker.

Evaluation of duty

The authors are concerned that there is little literature and a paucity of formal research with regard to duty teams. Out of office hours emergency duty teams (EDT) have been evaluated but not day duty services, despite their importance.

Section 3: Key characteristics of duty work

"Anyone who has never made a mistake has never tried anything new."

Albert Einstein (1879-1955)

Duty is the social services department's front-line: the front door. If work is not identified, diagnosed and actioned appropriately, the situation of children referred for help may become unsafe. All referrals, new and previously known, come first to the duty team; hence, an immediate diagnosis is required to identify the nature of the problem. Decisions are needed at the very first contact point about the degree of urgency, the degree of risk, and the degree of need.

Children in need

Referrals to social services are perceived as 'families and children in need'. They involve a variety of situations – from simpler, more straightforward matters, to very complex, higher risk matters: children found in the street or in the home alone; families without accommodation; without money; or without sufficient clothing. Children at risk of danger or significant harm will be identified through an initial assessment unless the case is immediately obvious, where an injury exists or where there is allegation and/or evidence of another abuse. As soon as any risk of significant harm is identified (Children Act 1989) a decision will be made as to the need for some form of professional and/or family discussion in the way of a strategy or planning meeting.

Agencies in the community are expected to undertake some initial work in clarifying the matter before automatically referring a child to social services. There are many occasions where a simple discussion with a parent may explain why the child was not picked up from school on time; or why the child appeared to be hungry or distressed; or why the parent gave the child a slap. There is a serious misunderstanding in some places that every incident must be referred to duty. The very clear exception is the occasion when a child has been or is likely to suffer serious hurt and where there may be a criminal offence involved. Then referral to social services and possibly police is necessary. These referrals nowadays are mostly undertaken on special interagency referral forms which need to be completed fully and accurately. These save a great deal of time and repetition of pursuing information with parents. Where there is the possibility of serious harm or danger, an investigation is likely. Hence the assessment becomes a Section 47 investigation.

Child protection

Child protection matters may include children involved in minor incidents such as being pushed over at school while at play, to major events with very severe injuries and traumatic experiences of abuse and assault. Sometimes duty staff are presented with family deaths and on rarer occasions even murder, and have to provide immediate management of the trauma and crisis for the children.

Many children are referred by police, school, family members, health professionals, independent agencies and, on occasion, anonymous callers. Overnight emergencies are referred the next morning by police and the emergency duty team /after hours team. The Section 47 investigation may lead to a child protection conference and the start of what the Assessment Framework calls a Core Assessment. The latter is an in-depth comprehensive assessment.

Not all referrals are emergencies

Not all referrals are emergencies or high-risk and complex. Thoburn, Wilding and Watson (2000) state that in the referrals involved in their study (712 children), just over half the referrals involved a request for general support or a specific service or other matters not seen as coming up in the framework of child protection.

Requests for practical information or documents are common. The following are typical: requests for birth certificates from those who have been in the care of a local authority; information for schools about children being assessed for special needs education; another local authority, now working with a family, requires information for court proceedings. Although not emergency or high-risk matters, they should be dealt with promptly.

The importance of the first contact

Requests for help require an immediate response. The duty worker's first contact with the referrer is critical in assessing all the clues about the meaning of the referral for the child involved. Does a child found wandering the street suggest something very serious about the parents' behaviour? What are the implications of homelessness; what is the state of the child's health; what is happening about schooling; is the family eligible for housing assistance? Does an anonymous call indicate a very serious situation or is it a vindictive neighbour? How best to respond to a pregnant thirteen year old who wants a termination without telling her mother?

Duty teams undertake the first stage of any complex referral requiring ongoing work. The staff member receiving the referral must be highly skilled in asking the right questions appropriately and in the analysis of the case. A recommendation for a service or for action will then be made, sometimes in consultation with the manager. Some cases are urgent, but all need immediate attention at this stage. The Assessment Framework scheme, recognising the necessity for speedy action, requires the manager's decision about a service response within 24 hours of the referral. The more accurate the initial information and early assessment, the more rapid the response. Whatever happens at this stage may affect whether the child and family are given the most appropriate service.

Tracking

Duty is the initial assessment process. Therefore the people who work in duty need to be able to think and act quickly, to be innovative and to manage a wide range of situations.

Keeping track of all referrals is a major part of any duty system. Without constant attention to the systems that process the work, and sound arrangements for the allocation of it, case files and papers can go missing and backlogs of all kinds build up. Workers become anxious and stressed and their assessments suffer. This can create particular problems with referrals previously unknown to the social services department.

Managing the desk and supervision

For the duty service, management of the duty desk and supervision are crucial. There are two forms of supervision characteristic of a duty service. The first involves the 'desk itself' and the monitoring of the process of incoming referrals. It includes the decisions made and the allocation of new referrals, and the coordination and supervision of the initial assessment. The second is the more traditional supervision of practice overview and development of the worker. Both forms of supervision have always been required for duty, but with the implementation of the Assessment Framework and the timing principles integral to that approach, it is now even more relevant. Add to this the skill mix of workers being used in some local authorities and it can be seen that it is essential to have clear and constant monitoring of the workflow.

Models for monitoring workflow

There are different managerial arrangements for monitoring the workflow in duty. In larger departments with two duty team managers, there may be a co-management arrangement. In others, the more traditional arrangement of a manager and an assistant team or practice manager may operate. There are advantages and disadvantages in both management arrangements and each model needs careful consideration. Constant supervision and monitoring of a duty desk is very demanding for a manager. It demands a high level of concentration and a capacity to deal with several matters at the same time. Exhaustion and burnout will occur without a relief arrangement. Without recognition of the danger of burnout in social work duty, managers may be unable to support and supervise staff adequately and a dangerous service for children may result. Where there is a manager and assistant team or practice manager, and the latter is expected to take the main responsibility for managing the desk, the demands can be excessive. The role for senior practitioners in duty needs careful thought; one of their responsibilities can be to assist in the management of the desk.

Generally, we prefer the co-management approach, where the managers manage the desk in rotation. The duty team is divided into two supervisee groups, but strategic and corporate tasks are shared. The important requirement of this arrangement is the need for close collaboration, communication, and a willingness to share and trust one another.

The rota

There is considerable discussion in duty teams about the most effective way of managing the workflow in the duty team. A number of good practice principles need to be borne in mind when determining the arrangements for the dispersal of referrals to workers. Accessible, open and available workers are required both at the point of first contact when the initial referral is made and the details taken. Then again the point of undertaking the Initial Assessment, and/or subsequent assessment such as the Section 47 investigation, and Core Assessment.

The next matter of importance is the completion of a speedy assessment in order to determine the nature of the service required. Finally, there is the question of whether a referral should be managed by one worker to the completion of the particular assessment, or whether the referral should be left to be handed on at the duty desk to whichever worker comes on rota next until completion.

Hence there is the matter of the rota, and the length of time workers should be on call. It appears that in some places workers are scheduled on duty for a day at a time, in other places two days on and three off (and vice versa) and in yet other places workers may be scheduled on duty for five days and then have five days off. In respect of the latter, the five days might start on a Tuesday or a Wednesday, so that there is a weekend off in between.

In the view of the writers, the strongly-preferred mode is the allocation on duty of the case for assessment to one worker for completion. This approach offers consistency of worker and task, clarity for the service user as to the identity of the worker, and certainly a speedier completion of assessment.

A number of authorities continue to leave the assessment in the action duty basket to be completed over time by a consecutive run of workers. This approach is less efficient in a number of ways. Service users are confused about who is dealing with their request for help; workers are not likely to be as committed to the task, given that they are undertaking a very limited part of the work and tend to do fragments of the tasks. The work overall is fragmented, the time taken to complete the assessment excessive and the quality of the assessment and report often not as good a standard as possible.

Whether a team decides to work its members on duty for the two or three days on/off or the five days on/off, this longer period on duty will certainly facilitate a greater chance of completion of the assessment task with better quality, with more speed and by one worker, than if the rota was one day on/off with the division of labour to complete the assessment. Certainly it is possible to have alternate days on duty rota, and have cases allocated to one worker for completion, but the worker's overall work time is very fragmented.

Essential duty work skills

Work on duty requires staff with highly developed attributes. Those essential are:

- communication skills
- the ability to network

- the ability to manage different work flows
- the ability to cope with the bombardment and the stress this can produce
- the ability to work in a team
- a liking for, and ability to, carry out crisis intervention.

Transfer or referring on

The duty team undertakes the initial work to assess the problem. If it requires extended social work it may be passed to a long-term team. In many authorities, there are criteria about how and when the child and the family should be transferred to a looked after team, children in need team or child protection/family support team.* This early work with parents and child sets the tone for future work. The attitude of the duty worker to the family and a good assessment may save hours later, and may facilitate a more cooperative contact between the subsequent worker and the family. Alternatively, the initial duty contact can alienate the family from the worker and the department as a whole.

A current problem may be the lack of capacity to accept new work in the long-term social work teams. Hence there may be a great deal of prevarication around the transfer process of cases from duty. As mentioned earlier in this booklet, the various parts making up the whole range of services in a department must work together. One of the most severe obstructions in the duty service is the accumulation of 'backlog' cases. These are referrals which should have been dealt with and closed or transferred to another more appropriate team. In order for the duty workers to sustain a rapid and appropriate completion of

---

* Common criteria for transfer point include: the first LAC statutory review; the first proceedings in court; the initial child protection conference.

the assessment and referral process, the arrangement for the transfer of cases must be clear, formal and regular. It is useful to prepare the relevant team in advance if at all possible, and certainly the negotiation of the transfer of cases should involve a process/meeting with a manager, with even a senior manager being present.

PART TWO: DEVELOPMENT

Section 4: Finding out what is going on

"Proverbial wisdom counsels against risk and change. But sitting ducks fare worst of all."

Mason Cooley (1927-)

Establishing what is actually happening

The operations of the duty team must be constantly monitored. Some aspects may be clear but others are not and it is unlikely that the whole picture is addressed. This is often due to day-to-day pressures and bombardment. There is a variety of information sources about the duty process to be checked; some of these are based on sound evidence, but others need to be checked and assessed for their reliability.

Key questions to be asked constantly include:

- is the service safe for children?
- are decisions safe?
- does the duty manager know what is in the duty basket?

A number of specific areas associated with the actual day-to-day practice of the duty team should be held in focus. These include the following twelve areas:

1. Order and chaos

Assess the relative order or chaos of the work arrangements in the team. Does it apply to all areas of the work or is it confined to special areas such as the intake of new referrals, the allocation of work, filing or the accuracy of recording and reports? Are the systems in place fit for current practice or are they designed for a different situation, time, work pattern or organisational structure?

2. The workflow system

The arrangements for work on referrals and enquiries must enable a minimum standard of good practice. The principles underpinning any arrangement in duty work include: accurate diagnosis; speedy decision-making for the appropriate service; rapid action; and the completion of the work, preferably by one worker.

The system should facilitate accurate recording of data on a computer information system, and accurate recording to enable tracking the case file or papers.

3. Timing

Making speedy decisions about the service required is central to good practice (Harding and Beresford, 1996). This is one of the key objectives of the Assessment Framework, which requires such decisions to be made within 24 hours of the referral date. Falling behind the Framework results in a backlog of work awaiting attention and decision-making.

4. Allocation

There is a need to pass work rapidly to staff for processing. Allocation of work on assessment on duty is different from that of a long-term team. The first level assessment, known as an Initial Assessment, with a brief intervention is the task of the duty team.

There is an art to selecting the most appropriate team member to take on work with particular families. It involves an awareness of the experience of each worker, her/his workload, interests and needs for professional development. Allocation of work within a team is a skilled task and the team manager needs to do this with the team. It can cause considerable problems if staff feel they are being given work unfairly. In our experience this difficult task can be aided by a teamload management system. However rudimentary, it should 'describe' the total work of the team and should give all members information about the total workload of their team and other staff (Rosen, 1999).

5. Threshold

Decisions about significant harm and the safety of children referred to a duty service for help must be robust, evidence based, clear and feasible. The assessment of circumstances and of significant harm and thresholds of safety can vary between different workers in a team, between different parts of the children and families services and between different organisations. Ongoing discussion within and between teams is required to obtain clarity and more consistent practice. There should be clear and accessible protocols about work in this anxiety-provoking area of social work, including those on working across different divisions of the department and between organisations (Kearney et al., 2000). There is also presently the 'refocusing' debate and questions as to the need to take a more comprehensive view of referred problems, without in any way minimising serious possibilities of harm for children where they exist. Social workers tend to explore most matters from a perspective of child abuse, rather than look to see what can be done to help the family manage better, where this might be more appropriate.

Thoburn et al. (2000) suggest that: "Authorities had guidelines about the priority given to cases, but there was confusion in the minds of some of the workers interviewed about the difference between criteria for crossing the 'in need' threshold and thus being eligible for services and the criteria for prioritisation. It was this latter set of guidelines on which workers appeared to be basing their decisions."

6. Eligibility

Managers must negotiate clear departmental eligibility criteria about those family difficulties that can be accepted for a social work service. They need to be regularly updated and accessible to all staff. Most departments now provide written criteria, but in our experience, there is still some confusion about the social services department's responsibility for financial support and accommodation/housing for families, and their responsibilities towards asylum seekers and 'overstayers'.

7. Quality of files, forms and reports

The points made here seem trivial, yet it is surprising how the quality of files and reports of a social services department reflect the standard of day-to-day practice. It is essential to get these practical written tasks right to maintain a high standard of practice and a commitment and application from workers in the duty team.

a) The quality of file or paper cover: we have found papers about families poorly-presented, held together or contained in an envelope of some kind, such as a plastic folder. Poorly-organised papers and files have a depressing effect on workers. If background information and referral papers are of poor quality, badly organised or confused, the worker feels an additional strain before the work with the family begins. This must impact on the duty worker's ability to work effectively, efficiently and appropriately with service users.

The retention and 'progress' of papers about referred children and families and the interventions planned to help them should be organised so that there is no risk of losing them. This may seem to be an obvious suggestion, but in our experience, it needs to be constantly restated. Establishing clear standards is not easy and requires expertise, hard work and commitment. However, it can be done and is essential to good social work practice (Rosen and Simmons, 2001).

b) **Tracking paperwork**: in departments with a substantial rate of new referrals, keeping track of papers and files is a central issue. Management needs to check the systems and ensure that a proper record is made of the location of records and papers. This can be achieved by a computer database, backed up by a simple manual paper tracking system as described earlier (see Appendix 1).

c) **The quality of referral information**: the Assessment Framework offers a useful initial referral format and its main headings appear in slightly different forms in different authorities. A common problem is a section not completed or poorly completed. Duty workers, whether qualified or not, sometimes find it difficult to obtain full details and important information required to identify the appropriate service. For example, details as basic as the full range of family surnames may be essential to trace previous involvement of the local authority with the family or an individual member. Changes of surname following a new spouse or partner may not be recorded; half-siblings may have different surnames from different fathers. Another frequent omission is information about the family's ethnicity or cultural background (see Thoburn et al., 2000). This may be critical to the understanding of a problem, and the identification of appropriate action and services. Workers have explained that they find these areas of initial enquiry sensitive and intrusive, and acknowledge that they may therefore avoid them.

Getting the balance between asking intrusive questions and ensuring that the child is safe may be difficult. Staff do need to be clear that the safety of children is their priority but may need further training and the support of more experienced staff if they are worried about asking 'impertinent' or 'intrusive' questions.

Basic principles of communication with families and children are fundamental when initiating the referral discussion. In particular, one should explain and give as much information as necessary about what one is doing and why. Respondents will be much more willing to give personal details if they know the purpose of questions. We need to remember too that the Assessment Framework requires the sharing of assessment reports with service users. Hence appropriate, open and professional contact with a service user early on is likely to contribute to a better process later.

8. Backlog of work awaiting management decisions

This is a very frequent problem, especially where there are large numbers of referrals. A substantial number of cases awaiting a decision on the next step, whether at points of intake or completion of the Initial Assessment or, indeed, Section 47 or Core reports, require immediate attention.

If essential decisions are held up due to day-to-day pressure of work, they not only delay progress but can also place a child at risk. The Assessment Framework scheme requires a decision on the initial referral enquiry within 24 hours. The completion of the Initial Assessment stage is expected in seven working days, and the manager must then check the worker's recommendation and decide on the next step. Thought needs to be given as to how to manage the process of decisions and allocation of work.

Regular and constant contact between team members and the manager is important in progressing the decision-making process. A team manager who is hands on has a facilitating effect on the worker making the decision. However, the duty team manager's own management needs to be aware that this style of working, although useful for staff, can be exhausting and may easily lead to burnout for the manager. This is why supervision and other support for duty managers is crucial.

9. Supervision: regularity and quality

Supervision of workers is imperative in every team and essential for competent decision-making. All social work is stressful but work on duty is particularly so (Morrison, 1993). However, in the duty team supervision is especially complex because of the speed of work and the frequent requirement to deal with crisis situations. Workers facing these situations need a good deal of daily support as well as the usual regular and planned supervisory sessions, usually offered at two or three weekly intervals.

When teams become busy, supervision is often the activity that is postponed first (Marsh and Triseliotis, 1996), but it is then that it is even more necessary.

One word of warning: however skilled the supervision, it can sometimes assume too much responsibility for both a good quality service and reducing worker stress. It cannot compensate for a lack of other necessary components of good practice such as opportunities for continuing professional development, decent pay scales and an office properly and suitably equipped to run a complex personal service.

10. Management information

Regular use of recorded information about referrals is essential in identifying:

- appropriate staffing establishments
- the nature of referrals for assessment
- the nature of re-referrals
- identification of cases and the worker responsible
- the skills needed and quality of work performance.

Monthly statistics required by the Department of Health are drawn from this information. Whilst managers have always used this information as part of their planning strategy, the regular use and integration of current computer software systems into their day-to-day work may be a new task to some of them (see Section 9 below).

Some departments have experienced difficulty and delay in integrating information required for efficient day-to-day practice into their present computerised systems. Computerised information systems should have the facility to record the start and close dates of the various assessment reports for the Assessment Framework, produce spreadsheets of relevant information on caseloads, and attach names of workers to cases.

Another common problem is accurate logging of data onto computer information systems. This task is usually undertaken by administrators and/or workers themselves. The accuracy and timing of recorded data will fundamentally affect the usefulness of computer information reports. Regular communication between practice teams and the organisation's technical computer unit is essential to facilitate systems for practice needs. Systematic and thorough training of staff about software and types of critical data is also essential.

The team manager and team members require information about the team's workload, the workflow and the characteristics of families being referred. Progress-chasing will give an indication of the degree of control the team has over its work and performance. This, of course, does not mean that all work will be allocated and completed to all timetables and work plans. However, we have found that actually knowing about the gaps can be the first stage in management information for some teams. Collecting the information and communicating it to others can be an energising experience for duty staff.

11. Team morale, sickness and worker turnover

Team morale is often reflected in the frequency and number of staff members on sick leave, especially long-term sick leave due to stress. Exit interviews with staff can indicate how workers feel about their work experience. Action is required to identify and remedy unreasonably high levels of stress and overwork and low morale within the team. Most inner city departments have very serious problems in obtaining well experienced, competent staff as well as newer and less experienced or qualified staff. A further problem is the balance between agency workers and permanent staff. Some inner city duty teams for children and families are staffed at least 50 per cent by agency social workers. Managers have to be sensitive about deploying their permanent staff, as workers who can be carrying out exactly the same social work tasks may be employed under quite different terms and conditions.

In a healthy team there is pleasant interaction and mutual assistance between all staff. Where there is low morale and dissatisfaction, some staff members will complain about 'unfair' allocation of work and other matters, even if it is not true.

12. What is a functioning, healthy team?

- A healthy team has the capacity to be mutually cooperative, supportive, courteous and helpful towards one other.

- There is a capacity for workers to encourage and motivate appropriate cooperation among themselves in social services and those in other community agencies.

- There is good communication and a partnership between workers and parents.

- There is trust between team members and openness to the implementation of change.

- The team has a capacity for learning, fostered by the organisational culture.

- The team can respond positively to criticism.

Section 5: Initiating Change

"People change and forget to tell each other."

Lillian Hellman (1905-1984)

Principles of change

Standards of duty work may have been assessed as unsatisfactory by an outside organisation such as the Social Services Inspectorate (SSI). Alternatively the social services department itself, through its own regulatory or quality development processes, has deemed the duty team as being in need of review and improvement.

The approach described in this booklet is one of many that can be adopted. The authors recommend it because it has been used effectively in a variety of different local authorities. Essentially the approach takes the principles of social work practice, those of good management and of the management of groups, and applies this mix to the development of the duty team within the organisation.

A change agent

Having identified the need for change, what is the driver for this change, or how should it be applied? The authors have been brought into organisations to assist management to identify problems, and to aid changes. Organisations do not necessarily require the help of outside consultants. The process outlined below can be, and has been, carried out by management staff within the agency or local authority. However, there does need to be somebody who has responsibility for activation and progress-chasing the agreed goals or targets. In this booklet this person is called the change agent. The change agent may be a manager, a staff development officer or trainer, or an outside consultant. The duty manager can be the change agent and, in any case, managers, together with teams, invigorate change and should always be essential activists in any change. However, it has been found to be helpful on occasions for someone from outside the team to act as a catalyst in a change process. If the latter is the case, they must work very closely with all staff.

The change agent – knowledge base and skills

The change agent, whether the team manager, another staff member or an external consultant, must:

- accept the principle that practice is not, and cannot be, a linear matter
- have understanding and experience of group dynamics
- understand organisational dynamics
- have clear communication skills
- model good practice and not be afraid to demonstrate social work practice at a variety of levels and complexity
- have faith and optimism about the team's ability to change and develop
- trust the staff's ability to work towards change and better practice
- be accessible
- be eclectic or holistic in his or her approach to change
- have a capacity to guide the development and learning capacity of staff through operational tasks.

The manager or change agent must also:

- believe that the staff of the duty team have the necessary information to make changes
- believe and demonstrate that the staff of the duty team have a major contribution to make to solutions
- believe that the solutions are there if one listens properly
- take into account that every team has its own 'persona' and culture and work with this as appropriate.

Other important factors are that:

- The change agent (manager, consultant or developer) does not arrive with pre-determined solutions (even if this were possible!).
- All solutions are developed within the context of departmental policy and practice.
- There is partnership with staff. This does not necessarily mean equal partnerships as very few partnerships are exactly equal.
- Research based or knowledge based solutions are sought. All development work needs to be carried out with access to relevant and up-to-date research findings. We have extended the concept of research evidence in our work with duty teams to use the term 'knowledge based evidence'. This incorporates other kinds of relevant knowledge as well as those described as 'pure research'. The extra information and knowledge comes from service users themselves, the professional wisdom of social workers, departmental policies, and the legal framework and its requirements.

It is also important to accept that:

- Effective change is not easy to achieve (Smale,1998).
- Organisational change is ongoing. It is a pathway rather than a completed journey. It is best viewed as a series of pathways or small journeys.

- Nothing is set in stone although there are markers and goals. Working to develop duty teams must mean adaptability and the ability of all staff sometimes to alter or adapt the pathway.

Section 6: Consolidating change

"Observe always that everything is the result of change and get used to thinking there is nothing nature loves so well."
Marcus Aurelius Antonius (121-180)

Getting to know the key people involved in the change

1. The team manager is crucial to any team change; get to know him or her but do not undermine the team manager's authority. This is a delicate balance.

2. Try to establish trust with all team members. Time spent with each team member on a fairly informal basis is important. This will enable you to identify the thought leaders and the underminers.

3. Do the 'job'. Take part in the work of the team but only with the team's direction and approval. This also provides an opportunity for modelling good practice. Most duty teams are currently understaffed and are pleased to have somebody extra to share out the work, especially on a busy day. 'Low level tasks' such as answering phones on the duty desk, or accompanying a new social worker in an interview, demonstrate that this is a consultant who is willing to be involved with the team's work and provides an opportunity to get to know about the work of the team on a 'nitty gritty' day-to-day basis.

4. Negotiate with all levels of management and keep senior officers well-informed of progress as well as obtaining their views.

5. If possible, talk with or survey a small number of service users. The waiting room or reception area can be used sometimes to meet and talk with them while they are waiting for an appointment.

Obtain management information

6. Obtain management information. This is a good indicator of the chaos or order of the team.

7. What is the nature of the workload management system in operation? Is it on computer and available? How accurate is the computer database? Ascertain how many cases are open on duty, how many cases are allocated and how many are in the unallocated 'pile'.

8. How many cases are awaiting a management decision before work can proceed? Check whether there are any 'secret' places where some cases are kept 'on ice'.

9. Carry out a systems check, including what are the intake arrangements, what are the tracking systems in place for knowing the stages of work on a case and the documentation about this work. It is important to have adequate and robust tracking systems in place in duty.

10. What are the arrangements for processing mail and the EDT referrals? Where do administrators fit into the systems?

11. Is the duty service open and accessible during lunch times and holiday periods?

The quality of practice

12. Discuss with staff their professional decision-making processes. Assess professional development activities and the needs of team members.

13. Determine the actual supervision in the team, both formal and informal. Explore what supervision exists for the team manager. Obtain the departmental policy on supervision. This will not necessarily be what is happening in practice but can provide a benchmark for expectations.

The pace and development of change

14. While obtaining all the information above, change will be happening. Just having an outsider in a team room and asking a few questions gets staff thinking about what they are doing and whether there may be a better way of doing it. Sometimes it can seem as though not much is happening but changes will actually happen quite quickly.

15. All sorts of external factors influence the pace at which a team will be able to make changes as well as their intrinsic capacity to make changes as a staff group. The presence of a change agent means that their employers have made a high priority of the development of practice in the team. The decision to employ and pay an outside consultant is not taken lightly by commissioning local authority managers.

16. If the standards of practice are poor, most staff are fully aware that this is the case and have often made considerable efforts to improve them. Obtaining the help of an outsider formally recognises that the team needs extra input. However, it is not always easy for the team to admit that it needs extra help and to have

its work scrutinised. For the team manager it can signal a personal failure to manage, but it is much more likely that the organisational systems in place may have hindered success.

Summarising the tools for implementing change

1. **Consultations**: for all the duty team but in particular the team manager.

2. **Hands-on work** that demonstrates to staff the practice expected and what is necessary to provide the best and safest service. Staff learn on the job all the time. This is why it is so important that for any efficient change to occur, learning, rather than survival, must be possible. Staff need to be able to think about their own and other people's work, and to work with experts and experienced staff so that they can improve their own practice. Being too busy to think has become an accepted part of duty practice.

3. **Meetings**: purposeful meetings where there is shared learning. Group supervision can be as important as normal individual one-to-one supervision. It does not replace individual supervision but contributes to it. Group supervision appears to have become less and less part of the routine of work experience in social services departments but it can be a crucial, valuable and efficient method of learning about one's work.

When introducing and assessing change some necessary considerations include:

*   Timing is all-important.
*   Preparation is needed with analysis and strategic discussion both up and down the management and staff hierarchy. Up and down and up again is the

recommended journey for change plans and, of course, across levels.

- Try to get agreement with all staff for any proposed changes through consultation, but staff sometimes need a gentle reminder that even though they have been consulted, the end decision may be somewhat different from their proposals.

- Staff will need preparation for any changes in systems. This can be handled through induction meetings, training in its traditional form and preparation meetings. Everybody needs to be prepared. Altering a duty system without preparing the switchboard staff, for example, will undoubtedly lead to difficulties and will hamper any change.

- Other organisations also need information to prepare them for social services changes in the duty system. All this preparation may be time-consuming and may seem to slow down an agreed process of change, but it is time well-spent.

- If a new system is to be introduced, agree a day when the changes will take place so that staff can work towards it.

Some warnings

- Change is a constant feature of organisations – probably too constant for most staff. New directives from the government and the need to improve often poor public services means that change will continue.

- Organisations can alter policy relatively quickly but practice takes longer to change (Brown,1996).

- Altering one part of an organisation may have sometimes unwelcome 'knock on' effects on other parts of it. For example, devising a clear system about appropriate work for a duty team can result in transfer of cases to longer-term teams becoming a more formal process. Social workers and, in particular, their managers in these teams may then have far less discretion about what they can and cannot accept.

• Nothing is 'set in stone'. New systems need to be nursed along and will need to be 'tweaked' or refined as they are tested out.

Section 7: Infrastructure: what needs to be in place for an effective duty system

"You cannot depend on your eyes when your imagination is out of focus."

Mark Twain (1835-1910)

Integrated systems in place that screen and gatekeep

Duty services must be underpinned by an infrastructure that will facilitate control of the workflow and its allocation. Often, especially in the larger, very disadvantaged boroughs of the bigger cities, the bombardment rate of referrals is overwhelming and chaos arises. If order and a tight rein are not present, referrals may be missed, files and papers mislaid and, above all, control lost over the duty desk and duty work.

The systems

There are a number of basic principles essential to ensure efficient intake and processing of new referrals:

- There must be a gate keeping/screening function at the receiving or first contact point of any referral or enquiry. The enquiry/referral must be fully assessed as to whether the response should be the giving of advice or information or whether it requires a social work service.

- There must be a recognised and accepted clear process for the intake of new referrals. Some models establish a 'first contact' group or team on duty. This group identifies the details of the child and the nature of the problem only. There will then be a recommendation for a service or not. Often information or advice given by this first contact group resolves the matter. It is in this group that a mix of skills, as mentioned earlier, is employed. This staff group complete an initial referral form. The intake team or first contact group also offers a very important gatekeeping or screening service, vital for big busy social services departments. If a social work service is required the referral, in this model, is passed to another social worker for the completion of an assessment. In a number of places, workers on the intake desk or first contact group also undertake the Initial Assessment along with the initial referral.

- Our experience is that the model best suited to the big, heavily bombarded urban departments is that with a division of labour between intake and completion of assessment.

- The intake or duty team must have immediate access to a duty manager, and/or a senior practitioner. The principle of referring to the manager is to ensure that matters of consequence are not lost at the first contact point. Workers in mixed skill intake teams, including specialist workers, need to be conscious of the limitations of their professional role and expertise and should not hesitate to discuss matters with their manager.

- The location of the intake or duty team, its functions, arrangement and equipment should be planned. Other dimensions of this include the spatial seating arrangements, the positioning of the administrative support staff and the way in which the baskets for the paper-work are located and physically processed. Work on this aspect of duty has been carried out by Regan and Thorpe at Lancaster University (Regan, 1999; Thorpe, 1997). Regan says: "Most organisational change assumes that work falls into discrete functional areas and as a consequence little regard is given to the importance of spatial arrangements, technology and social relationships which are unique to particular contexts of activity."

- Staff of the duty team have to have knowledge about the other teams within the social services department as well as the external agents with whom it must work. Strategy and planning meetings are held by the duty team and a range of other professionals attend. Police, teachers and health personnel are frequent visitors, or should be.

- Data should be logged on the computer database as soon as possible after receipt of a referral. This includes a check as to whether the family/child is already known to the social services department, and whether it is currently an 'open case'. This logging process may be supported by a manual tracking system, as many computer programmes are still not sophisticated enough to sustain accurate data or, and more likely, data is not recorded accurately. At present, many of the software systems have a range of incompatibilities with the data collection needs of the Assessment Framework.

- Easy to access and up-to-date information must be available to managers, administrative and social work staff. This facilitates the appropriate allocation of referred families and children. It also provides the manager with management information about the caseload weighting for all workers, the referral rate in any period, along with data for the monthly statistics now required by the Department of Health. Local authority computer information systems vary in capacity and age. Some of the earlier systems are less flexible than more recently developed systems, and much negotiation is required internally to adjust the database to accept material which is now required to fit the Assessment Framework and other databases. Simple things like opening and closing dates for a case and naming the social worker carrying a case 'on duty' can cause immense problems for old IT systems. As a result, manual tracking sheets are used in some places to back up the computer database.

• The duty team may also be seen as the problem-solvers for a range of other matters: many switchboards put inappropriate calls through to duty believing that they can sort them out and callers, who want to talk to social workers in other teams who are unavailable, are often referred to duty. Problems completely unrelated to social work are often referred too. When the central switchboard knows the exact function of the duty team, it can then transfer telephone calls and other enquiries to the appropriate locations. The difference this can make to the calm of a duty room has to be seen to be believed.

Administrative staff

• Effective use of administrative staff underpins the duty systems. Mostly, administrative staff allocated to a duty team are accountable to two managers – the administrative line supervisor/manager and the social work duty manager. All allied staff need to comprehend the core business of any department, but are rarely given the induction required in order to identify their role in it (Rosen, 1999). The loyalty and first responsibility of administrative staff is to their organisation but in the duty team their purpose is to provide an effective service, however 'removed' they may perceive their work to be from the front-line. Administrative staff need to understand their importance in delivering the service, otherwise they may lead professional lives connected with, but independent of, the duty team. At its extreme, administrative staff may undermine its work. When President John Kennedy was touring NASA and asked a man in a corridor wearing overalls holding a broom what he did at NASA, he received the reply, "I work here to put men on the Moon".

- Administrative systems for tracking, allocating and referring on are crucial. The workflow system appropriate to a particular team is determined by a number of characteristics which relate to the nature of the service required and cover the demographic characteristics of the target population, the size of the team and the rate of demand for a service. In smaller, more isolated locations, division of labour may be unnecessary, and intake workers will manage referral calls as well as undertaking assessments. In cities with a large number of complex cases, major ethnic diversity and a transient population, chaos around the duty desk is common unless there are clear systems in place. In these locations it is worth considering a division of labour between servicing the initial call, and assessment and processing.

- The term 'duty desk' may refer to the intake desk and/or the desk taking duty referrals. In some models, as stated above, there will be only incoming referrals. In others, referrals may be received and possibly worked on by the same worker. The supervisory approach of managers of the duty desk is especially important. The manager and/or senior practitioner should be readily accessible for appropriate professional discussion, guidance and organisational advice. The location of the manager/senior practitioner is therefore important and is even more critical if the intake team has unqualified or young, inexperienced social workers. Much professional learning takes place in the workplace, especially in duty social work. In his research Michael Eraut found that 80 per cent of professional learning takes place in the work setting (Eraut, 1998). For duty and intake work, we think it is almost 100 per cent.

The organisation and processing of the duty 'basket' and workflow

- Managers must have knowledge and control of all work being referred. It is at the referral point that managers will identify the unsafe cases. Control of the work is lost where the bombardment rate is high or work is not clearly processed and in delineated places, even in less busy offices.

- Managers should have methods of identifying and tracking work and who is undertaking it. This can be done in a variety of ways and there are a number of personal styles. However, too many styles or too disparate a style among managers of the duty team will cause problems for staff. Any system must indicate the number and names of cases a worker holds, date of allocation and the start and close date of the assessment. The outcome should be recorded.

- 'Baskets' on the duty desk must be minimised and clearly located and labelled, so that everybody knows exactly what is in them. They will form part of the flow of the paper through the intake, assessment and referral processes within the team. While nothing about social work is likely to be linear, this is one area of work in which a clear and linear approach will be an advantage.

Unallocated cases

A major problem in big city departments is the chronic shortage of social workers. Frequently teams do not have their full complement of staff and it is difficult to allocate new work. The accumulation of 'unallocated' cases can cause enormous concern and may seriously obstruct the flow of work. Responses to blockages of this kind include occasional 'blitzes' on backlogs using workers on overtime, or bringing in external workers. Another useful approach is to use supervisory sessions to plan the completion of old cases by setting firm action plans and dates for completion. Duty work is not long term, and workers preferring to work on long-term casework should be encouraged to move to more appropriate teams.

Transfer from duty

Eligibility criteria for passing work over to other teams should be clearly established with formal transfer meeting handovers, after:

- the first statutory review (if child is accommodated or brought into care of the authority)
- the first child protection conference
- the first hearing in any situation where court proceedings are initiated.

There are a variety of successful ways in which cases may be passed to other teams. However, in many departments transfer of work can lead to tension between teams, caused by overwork and the strains and pressures of staff shortages. Whilst these problems continue, a list of unallocated work may be necessary, even though undesirable, and a constant review of these cases is essential. This can be done by continual prioritisation, looking at the risk to each child, regular focussed checks with the family and keeping them updated about the situation.

PART THREE: REVIEW

Section 8: Developing practice

"If everybody is thinking alike then somebody isn't thinking."
General G.S.Patton (1885-1945)

Developing the skills of workers

Improving practice standards is constant and ongoing, but how to do it, and continue to maintain enthusiasm and commitment to improvements, can be difficult. Set out below are what we have found helpful in assisting the improvement of practice. These findings are particularly relevant for duty staff but could equally apply to other specialties. Our findings are not 'rocket science' discoveries. Even if known to staff and managers, and they nearly always are, they need to be re-stated, re-visited and re-used.

1. A learning organisation

First and foremost is a culture of learning and change. Senior managers are crucial in promoting this and in setting an example by their own behaviour. They need to be willing to facilitate professional development for staff so that workers are motivated to view their practice critically, and to participate in development opportunities.

A learning organisation incorporates and supports a varied range of learning activities (Pottage and Evans, 1994). Many of them do not require a large input of financial resources. Managers, themselves, need to learn to exploit a number of 'on-the-job' situations which lend themselves to creating a learning and developmental environment. Such situations may include: action-learning sets, case presentations in team meetings, inviting speakers from other organisations or specialties and group supervision sessions. They can cover specific areas of practice such as thresholds in child protection, eligibility criteria for services or quality recording. Team members may identify wider issues for professional practice development, such as effective work with families, assessing children or effective social work intervention. We have found that these professional practice seminars work best if a case presentation approach is used.

2. The manager as teacher

In the social work profession the manager should also be a teacher or trainer. We consider that some managers have neglected their teaching role over the last few years, perhaps because they are busy with budgets and implementing policy change. However, teaching and passing on expertise is central to being a competent manager and can be one of the most rewarding aspects of the job. There are a range of approaches to teaching. The use of team meetings for case presentations and discussion is one way, informal discussion and consultation is another.

3. Supervision

Regular and constructive supervision improves practice. Most social services departments now have a supervisory policy and a requirement for regular supervision, covering specific aspects of practice.

Critical to the improvement of practice is the manager's skill in helping staff to identify strengths and weaknesses, areas of expertise and interest, and where they need to focus for learning and development. This knowledge can be applied in the allocation of work.

4. Inducting new staff

Managers have expressed concern about pressures placed on recently qualified workers. Staff shortages in some departments have resulted in inexperienced workers undertaking work with very complex cases. There is a similar problem with workers brought in from other countries to fill staffing gaps. Managers have to undertake a training role with these workers with a need for frequent consultation and guidance. Demands on the manager to induct staff reduce time for their other duties and they often feel excessively pressured.

Staffing problems are now being recognised and strategies are being developed to overcome them. There are ways of managing these difficulties and, in our view, they can be applied generally, irrespective of staff shortages.

Induction pack

An induction pack should be available which gives information about the department and especially, the range of policies and protocols essential to the management of practice. Included in the pack should be:

- eligibility criteria for services
- policies on child protection procedures
- a short description of the core business of every team.

New staff should be taken through the induction pack, and for staff from other countries, some sessions on the Children Act and its main principles, and the Assessment Framework, must be provided.

In addition induction can be an excellent developmental opportunity for an experienced or senior practitioner as it gives them a chance to review current policy and practice.

Day-to-day support

In the induction period new staff can benefit from sharing cases and shadowing an experienced worker. Practical tasks can be given to them and can relieve some of the pressure of work for the experienced worker. **Work patterns learned at the beginning of a social worker's career are crucial in setting the standard for continued practice.**

5. Mentoring

Mentoring is another approach useful to many workers and may be undertaken with the team as a whole, or individually. Mentoring can be provided by staff within the department or by bringing in an outside practitioner. It can take a number of forms, but is usually best when it focuses on specific areas of interest and need. Group mentoring, rather like case discussions, can be enormously helpful and may also facilitate consistency in decision-making and quality.

6. Action-learning sets

It may be possible to help small groups of staff establish action-learning sets which can focus on particular areas of interest. This can work well across teams, given that some initial energy is put into motivating staff and some collective negotiating with other managers.

7. Performance indicators

The implementation of central government requirements has led to considerable changes in the ways in which practice is monitored and developed. The latest, for children and families work, is the Assessment Framework that contributes to government's performance indicators (PIs). The timeframes set for the Initial Assessment and the Core Assessment are based on good practice and research.

Making standards relevant to practice

Departments have to help staff embed new standards into good practice. Many workers are sceptical about what they see as a bureaucratic exercise, assume they are just form-filling and take a box filling approach (Rosen and Simmons, 2001). Managers need to emphasise that the Assessment Framework is a valuable tool in the initial assessment. The basic principles in interviewing and making assessments are:

- respect for the child and family
- explain what the family and department need to know
- identify their perception of the problem
- appropriate discussion within their comprehension
- sensitive listening
- talk with the child
- an analysis
- a plan of action.

Thoburn, Wilding and Watson (2000) suggest: "All assessments should conclude with a clear statement of the sort of behaviour that is causing concern and the type of harm or impairment to health or development that either has been caused or is likely to be caused. An estimate of the significance of this harm or impairment and the likelihood of it continuing is also necessary."

The quality of practice can be enhanced by appropriate use of the Assessment Framework. Use it as a guide to identify areas appropriate to the service user's needs. Complete the assessment forms in the most comfortable way for the service user. Some people will be very uncomfortable about a form being completed in their presence, but others may be interested in seeing the form and, indeed, the scheme requires that they should be offered a copy in due course.

The analysis of the assessment should be informed by contemporary theory and research. The analysis provides the basis for a service plan. It is often omitted but is basic to a good assessment. A critical message to workers is that the Assessment Framework aids the quality of practice, communication with the service user, and the production of a sound analysis. It allows a clearer picture of social work response to referrals for management as well as providing performance indicators for the Department of Health.

Aldgate and Statham (2001) conclude that "prevention" is likely to be easier and more cost effective than "cure", though both are needed. Clearly, careful assessment is needed to identify which children might benefit from early intervention. The research recommends that:

- It is important to assess and prioritise the children most at risk of impairment or significant harm for complex services that may be long-term.
- It is equally important to identify children and families who can respond positively to well targeted supportive services at an earlier stage.

Section 9: Management Information

"Discovery consists of seeing what everybody has seen and thinking what nobody has thought."

Albert Szent-Gryogyi (1893-1986)

The modernisation agenda

This government's modernisation agenda has produced performance indicators and requires the collection of statistics for regular reporting to the Department of Health. Management information has always been part of the manager's toolbox but unfortunately the new requirements are often seen as yet another bureaucratic chore, and separate from general day-to-day management tasks. They are often competed in a rush just before the deadline.

Integral to daily work

Management information should be integrated into the daily work of management and used to assist managers and their teams to effectively plan their work. It is essential to have on hand accurate information about: the nature of the work; the workloads of staff; the quality of service delivered with response times; the types of service needed and given; and, if possible, views from service users about their degree of satisfaction.

Thoburn, Wilding and Watson (2000) state: "If available resources are to be used to the best effect and if cases are to be made for further resources, information is needed about the sorts of families seeking assistance and the volume and nature of the different types of services needed."

For example, the adequacy of staffing numbers can only be assessed if the manager has accurate statistics about the volume and nature of the workload. A listing of all the activities being carried out by staff assists in a fairer distribution of the work. The same list can be used in supervisory sessions to help workers to assess their work and progress, to plan action and to identify training and development needs.

Good practice and service development needs:

• A range of data. This should be integrated into daily tasks as described in Section 7 of this booklet on infrastructure. The team manager is responsible for management information systems but some information gathering and analysis will be undertaken by administrative staff, and on occasions by social work staff.

• Appropriate spreadsheets and software systems negotiated with computer systems staff. Information should be printed off for periodic review by the manager. Caseload information may be needed weekly whilst other data, such as numbers of new referrals and child protection cases, may only be required monthly. Once this material becomes available regularly and is made accessible it is enormously valuable in day-to-day work. It also prevents panics when senior staff require specific data for strategic meetings or planning purposes. As Aldgate and Statham (2001) state about the research: "The overarching message is that the provision and delivery of services for children and families has made considerable progress under the Children Act, but there remains a need to refine systems, management and practice to use the Act even more effectively and to safeguard and promote the welfare of children in need."

Section 10: Summary of findings

The findings of this booklet are summarised below:

1. Ensuring that children are safe is the primary aim of the duty social work team. This applies to all staff, whatever their roles and responsibilities within the team.

2. All social work teams need to work towards providing a good standard of service. This is particularly important for the duty team as it is the first port of call for referrals and therefore sets a standard for the whole department.

3. Duty social work practice is guided by the Assessment Framework scheme. This scheme promotes the principles of good practice, including a focus on speedy, good quality assessments and service planning.

4. Duty systems should be constantly monitored and reviewed. Innovative approaches should be considered to sustain effective and efficient services.

5. Inappropriate or poorly sustained systems in duty may lead to chaos. Chaos can become comfortable and staff resistant to change. This can be dangerous.

6. Systems for monitoring and tracking the workflow on duty need to be appropriate for the service and the requirements of the social services department. In

identifying a model, the demography and geography of the area or location should be taken into account.

7. Duty social work requires a range of expertise. This includes clear planning of assessments. Good skills in communication, negotiation and diagnosis and techniques for rapid responses are needed in other social work specialities but are particularly important for duty staff.

8. Departmental computer software systems must be adapted for required data. Data must be accurately recorded on both computer and manual tracking systems.

9. Managers must have knowledge and control of the work referred to duty and the outcome. Frequent consultation is essential. The nature of supervision in duty is special to this work. There must be direct supervision on the 'duty desk' as well as the regular, planned traditional staff supervision sessions.

10. As in all social work but particularly in duty work, information about workflow should be in daily use. This is in addition to the social services department's performance indicators about services.

11. Improving practice is a constant. A learning organisation incorporates a range of learning activities including induction, on-the-job practice development, supervision, mentoring and action-learning.

12. Practice must be knowledge based.

13. Organisational change is ongoing and should reflect the needs of the service user. It should also be planned with, and owned by, staff.

14. All teams in a social services department are interdependent. Transfer of work between teams should occur through agreed and clear protocols.

15. Duty staff have to make speedy but safe decisions. They should have clear criteria about eligibility for service, knowledge about children and families in need and an understanding of key practice concepts such as significant harm and risk management.

And finally:

Community based agencies are integral to the effective work of social services. The Area Child Protection Committee (ACPC) and other associated organisations together with social services have responsibility for the provision of services to children and families. Communication and cooperation are essential to an understanding of the contribution of each organisation to the overarching purpose – the well-being of all children.

References

Aldgate, J. and Statham, J. (2001) *The Children Act Now: Messages from research 2001*, London: The Stationery Office

Brown, J. (1996) *Chance Favours the Prepared Mind*, London: HMSO

Department of Health, Department for Education and Employment, Home Office (2000) *Framework for the Assessment of Children in Need and their Families*, London: The Stationery Office

Eraut, M. (1998) "Managers hold the key to developing knowledge and skills", *Professional Manager*, March

Harding, T. and Beresford, P. (1996) *The Standards We Expect: What service users and carers want from social services workers*, London: NISW

Kearney, P., Levin, E. and Rosen, G. (2000) *Alcohol, Drug and Mental Health Problems: Working with families*, London: NISW

Marsh, P. and Triseliotis, J. (1996) *Ready to Practise?* Aldershot: Avebury

Morrison, T. (1993) *Staff Supervision in Social Care*, Harlow: Longman

McCaughan, N. and Palmer, B. (1994) *Systems Thinking for Harassed Managers*, London: Karnac

Pottage, D. and Evans, M. (1994) *The Competent Workplace*, London: NISW

Regan, S. (1999) *Transformation in the Organisation of Social Work in the Public Sector*, PhD thesis, Lancaster University

Rosen, G. (ed) (1999) *Managing Team Development*, London: NISW

Rosen, G. and Simmons, L. (2001) *Making the Best Use of Standards*, London: NISW

Smale, G. (1998) *Managing Change Through Innovation*, London: The Stationery Office

Taylor, G. (1999) *Managing Conflict*, London: Directory of Social Change

Thoburn, J., Wilding, J. and Watson, J. (2000) *Family Support in Cases of Emotional Maltreatment and Neglect*, London: The Stationery Office

Thorpe, D. (1997) *Dealing with Child Care Telephone Referrals: Reflexive practice for duty/intake social workers and supervisors*, Paper presented at the CCETSW Learning for Competence Workshop 1997

APPENDICES

Appendix 1: Example of a Manual Tracking Sheet

Name, DOB of child	Case ID. Number	CIN Code	Priority	Nature of case	Named social worker	Start initial assessment	Close initial assessment	Start sect. 47 investigation	Close sect. 47 investigation	Outcome
								Investigate Joint/Single		
Smith, Alison 27-08-1991	77467	4	1	Mother mental health, drug dependency, child managing issues	Jackson, Yvonne	12-10-2001	17-10-2001			Family support identified – mother in treatment

Appendix 2: Suggested Models for Assessment and Referral Team (Duty Team)

Model 1

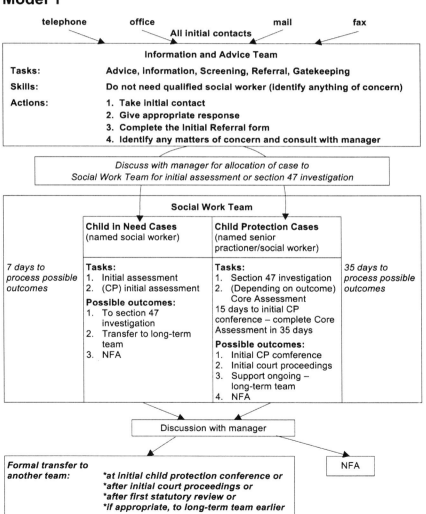

telephone   office   mail   fax

All initial contacts

Information and Advice Team

Tasks:	Advice, information, Screening, Referral, Gatekeeping
Skills:	Do not need qualified social worker (identify anything of concern)
Actions:	1. Take initial contact
	2. Give appropriate response
	3. Complete the Initial Referral form
	4. Identify any matters of concern and consult with manager

Discuss with manager for allocation of case to
Social Work Team for initial assessment or section 47 investigation

Social Work Team

Child in Need Cases
(named social worker)

Child Protection Cases
(named senior practioner/social worker)

7 days to process possible outcomes

Tasks:
1. Initial assessment
2. (CP) initial assessment

Possible outcomes:
1. To section 47 investigation
2. Transfer to long-term team
3. NFA

Tasks:
1. Section 47 investigation
2. (Depending on outcome) Core Assessment
15 days to initial CP conference – complete Core Assessment in 35 days

Possible outcomes:
1. Initial CP comference
2. Initial court proceedings
3. Support ongoing – long-term team
4. NFA

35 days to process possible outcomes

Discussion with manager

Formal transfer to another team:
*at initial child protection conference or
*after initial court proceedings or
*after first statutory review or
*if appropriate, to long-term team earlier

NFA

Model 2

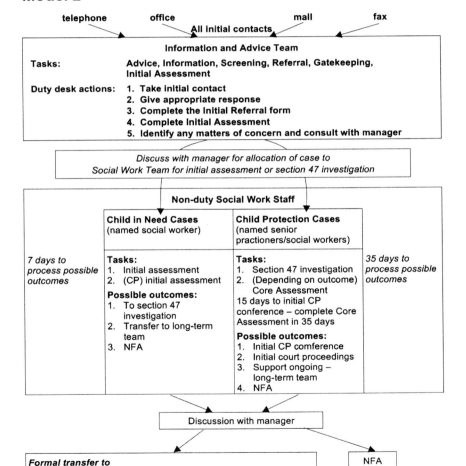

telephone   office   mail   fax

All initial contacts

Information and Advice Team

Tasks:	**Advice, Information, Screening, Referral, Gatekeeping, Initial Assessment**
Duty desk actions:	**1. Take initial contact**
	2. Give appropriate response
	3. Complete the initial Referral form
	4. Complete initial Assessment
	5. Identify any matters of concern and consult with manager

Discuss with manager for allocation of case to
Social Work Team for initial assessment or section 47 investigation

Non-duty Social Work Staff

7 days to process possible outcomes	**Child in Need Cases** (named social worker)	**Child Protection Cases** (named senior practioners/social workers)	*35 days to process possible outcomes*
	Tasks: 1. Initial assessment 2. (CP) initial assessment **Possible outcomes:** 1. To section 47 investigation 2. Transfer to long-term team 3. NFA	**Tasks:** 1. Section 47 investigation 2. (Depending on outcome) Core Assessment 15 days to initial CP conference – complete Core Assessment in 35 days **Possible outcomes:** 1. Initial CP comference 2. Initial court proceedings 3. Support ongoing – long-term team 4. NFA	

Discussion with manager

Formal transfer to another team:	*at initial child protection conference or* *after initial court proceedings or* *after first statutory review or* *if appropriate, to long-term team earlier*

NFA